THE JEWISH CHILDREN'S BIBLE

EXODUS

Adapted by Sheryl Prenzlau

PITSPOPANY

NEW YORK ◆ JERUSALEM

The Israelites were happy to give gifts for the mishkan.

Published by Pitspopany Press
Text copyright © 1997 by Sheryl Prenzlau
Illustrations copyright © 1997 by Zely Smekhov, Lena Guberman

Design: Benjie Herskowitz

PITSPOPANY PRESS books may be purchased for educational or special sales by contacting:
Marketing Director, Pitspopany Press, 40 East 78th Street, New York, New York 10021.
Fax: 212 472-6253.

ISBN: 0-943706-32-7

Printed in Hungary

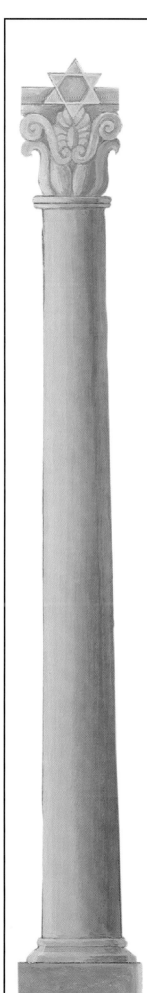

Contents

Slaves In Egypt

שמות

A new king arose in Egypt.

This Pharaoh said to his people, "The Children of Israel are becoming too many. Soon there will be more of them than us. Let's think of a way to destroy them, because if we are attacked by any of our enemies, who knows? Perhaps the Children of Israel will turn against us and help our enemies!"

So Pharaoh decided to make the Israelites into slaves. In this way, the Children of Israel would be poor and weak, much too weak to rebel against the Egyptians. Special watchmen called taskmasters were appointed to watch over the Israelites. They were mean and cruel men, and made the Israelites work from morning until night, building cities from bricks. The Israelites even had to make their own bricks from mud and straw!

The two biggest cities they built were called Pitom and Ramses.

The Egyptians were sure that if they made life really terrible for the Israelites then they would not want to have children.

But the more the Egyptians and their taskmasters made life miserable for the Israelites, the more the Israelites became fruitful and multiplied.

This scared the Egyptians, so they made the Israelites work harder and harder, until it was almost impossible for anyone to work any harder. But still the Israelites kept having babies.

Then the king spoke to the nurses who helped the Israelite women when they gave birth, for in those days everyone gave birth at home.

"When you see that an Israelite woman has given birth to a baby boy, I command you to kill the baby at once. You must do this because I have been told by my magicians that a baby boy will be born to the Israelites who will lead them out of Egypt. I will not allow this to happen!" Pharaoh roared.

The nurses were afraid of the king, but they were even more afraid of God. They knew God was watching over the Israelites so they didn't obey Pharaoh. Instead of killing the baby boys, they helped the mothers hide them from the Egyptian soldiers.

When the king found out that the nurses had not obeyed his command, he was furious and called them back to his palace.

"What have you done?" he bellowed. "There are more baby boys than ever before!"

"Please, Your Highness," one of them cried. "We would have done what you said, but each time we came to a home where a baby was born, the mother had already given birth, and hidden the baby from us. We looked everywhere, but we couldn't find the Israelite babies."

God rewarded the nurses for saving the Israelite children, and made them and their families very wealthy.

Of course, the king was not happy. He needed a new plan, one that would rid him of the Israelite baby boys once and for all. He had an idea. He sent out a letter to the people in all the towns and cities of Egypt.

The Pharaoh commands all his subjects to spy on the Israelites. When you see an Israelite woman has given birth to a baby boy, you must kill him at once. But do not harm the baby girls.

This is the command of Pharaoh, your king.

And the Egyptian people hurried to do the king's command.

Moses Is Born

There was an Israelite woman named Yocheved who gave birth to a baby boy. She was able to hide her baby for three months. But when the Egyptians started searching all the Israelite houses, she knew she would have to do something quickly if she wanted to save her baby. So one day, Yocheved went out and cut some reeds that grew along the Nile River. From these reeds she wove a basket and covered it with tar on the outside and with clay on the inside so that it would stay dry. Then she placed her baby into the basket and pushed it into the middle of the water where the current took the basket downstream.

"Follow the basket, Miriam," Yocheved told her daughter. "See what happens, and who finds the basket." Miriam stood in the reeds and watched the basket float down the river.

When Pharaoh's daughter came down to the river to bathe, she saw the basket.

"Look, there's a basket," the princess told her servants. "I wonder what's inside?" The princess stretched out her hand and pulled the basket close to her. "There is a baby boy in here!" she exclaimed. "He is probably an Israelite boy. His mother must have put him in here. I will need someone to nurse him," she told those around her.

Hearing this, Miriam came out of her hiding place. "I'm sure I can find a woman to nurse him," she told the princess.

"That's wonderful!" said the princess. "Go at once."

Miriam ran home and brought her mother to the princess.

"Nurse this baby for me," the princess told Yocheved, "and I will pay you. When the child is old enough, bring him to the palace."

Yocheved was thrilled to have her baby back. She nursed the boy until he was old enough to go to the palace. When she brought him to the princess, the princess said, "From now on he will be my son. I will give him a new name — Moshe!"

The name Moshe means "to take out of the water." Today, many people use his English name, Moses.

Moses Meets The Israelites

At the palace, Moses was told that he was an Israelite whom the princess had saved from certain death. He was also reminded of how lucky he was to live in a palace and to be treated as an Egyptian instead of an Israelite slave.

When Moses was almost grown up, he became curious about his people. So he went to see for himself what kind of life they led.

Everywhere he went he saw the Israelites working very hard as slaves. He saw the Egyptian taskmasters forcing Israelites to work faster and faster, shouting at them and whipping them until they fell. Moses became angrier and angrier at what he saw.

One day, he came upon a taskmaster hitting an Israelite. Although Moses told him to stop, the taskmaster just whipped the Israelite harder and harder until it looked as though he would surely die. Moses looked around to see if anyone was watching and then hit the taskmaster with all his might. The Egyptian fell to the ground and died. Moses buried him in the sand and ran back to the palace as fast as he could.

The next day Moses went back and saw two Israelites fighting each other. "Stop this fighting, at once!" he commanded them.

"Who are you to tell us what to do?" one of the Israelites shouted. "Are you going to kill us like you killed the Egyptian?"

When Moses heard this, he knew that his secret was out. It would only be a matter of time before Pharaoh discovered that he had killed an Egyptian and then he would be sent to jail — or worse!

Moses ran away from the palace, into the desert. He had to hide from Pharaoh.

Moses Finds A Wife

Moses went to the land of Midyan. One day he was sitting near a well, when seven sisters came to draw water for their father's sheep. The other shepherds at the well wouldn't let the sisters water their sheep, and began to chase them away.

"Wait! I will help you," Moses called out to the sisters. He stopped the other shepherds from bullying the girls and helped them water their sheep. As soon as the animals finished drinking, the sisters thanked Moses and returned home.

"Why are you home so quickly?" their father, Yitro, asked. He knew that the girls usually had to wait a long time before the other shepherds let them water the sheep.

"An Egyptian helped us water the sheep," they answered.

"And where is this man?" their father inquired. "Call him here, so I can thank him and give him something to eat."

The sisters brought Moses to their father. Yitro liked Moses and invited him to stay with his family. Eventually, Moses married one of Yitro's daughters, Tzipporah. They called their first son Gershom, because the word *ger* in Hebrew means stranger, and although life was peaceful and good for him right now, Moses felt like a stranger in a strange land.

Not long after, important news arrived: The Pharaoh was dead. A new king ruled over Egypt. This new Pharaoh didn't want to punish Moses for what he had done. But like the previous king, he didn't like the Israelites. He made them work harder than ever.

The Israelites cried and prayed to God, asking that a leader be sent to them, someone who would take them out of Egypt and set them free.

God heard their prayers.

The Burning Bush

One day, Moses was in the desert, watching over Yitro's sheep. Suddenly, Moses looked up and saw a bush burning nearby. He watched the fire trying to burn up the bush, but the bush remained unharmed.

This is the strangest sight I have ever seen, Moses thought, as he moved closer to the bush. Just then, he heard his name being called.

"Moses! Moses!" the voice said.

"Here I am," Moses answered, looking around.

"Do not come closer," the voice said. "Take off your shoes because this is a holy place."

Moses did as he was told.

"I am the God of your father," the voice told him, "the God of Abraham, the God of Isaac, and the God of Jacob. My people are crying out for help. It is time to take them out of Egypt into a good land, filled with milk and honey. I have chosen you to go to Pharaoh, to take My people, the Children of Israel, out of Egypt."

"Who am I to talk to a Pharaoh?" Moses asked. "How can I take the Children of Israel out of Egypt?"

"You will not do this alone," God answered. "I will be with you. For just as the fire does not burn up this bush, so will you be able to do what I command you without being harmed by anyone.

"Go to the leaders of the Jewish people, and tell them that the God of their fathers has sent you to save them from the Egyptians. Then go with them to the king of Egypt and tell him that God has commanded the Israelites to worship in the desert for three days."

"But why should the leaders believe me?" Moses asked. "They will not believe that God spoke to me."

"They will listen to you when you show them these signs," God assured him. "Now take your shepherd's staff and throw it down on the ground," God commanded Moses.

The minute he threw it down, the staff turned into a snake.

Moses jumped back.

"Now pick it up by the tail," God told him. Moses picked up the snake by the tail, and it became a staff again.

"Put your hand into your shirt," God ordered Moses. Moses did as he was told. "Now take it out," God said. When he took out his hand it was white as snow. "Put back your hand and then take it out again," God said. Moses did as he was commanded. When he took out his hand from his shirt, it was back to normal.

"If the leaders still don't believe you after you have given them these signs, take some water out of the Nile River and pour it onto the ground. When the water hits the ground it will turn into blood."

But Moses still did not feel he should go. "I am not a public speaker, God," Moses said. "Sometimes I even stutter."

"Who makes a man speak, or hear, or see? Isn't it I?" God reminded him. "I will go with you and help you speak."

"Please God," Moses pleaded, "send someone else."

God was not happy with Moses' answer. "Your brother Aaron will meet you as you come to Egypt. If you do not wish to speak, then he will speak to the people for you, and I will tell you what to say to him."

Pharaoh Gets Angry

Moses went to Egypt and met Aaron on the way, just as God had told him. Together they went to the leaders of the Jews, showed them the signs, and then went to speak to Pharaoh.

"I do not know your God!" Pharaoh screamed at them. "The problem is that you Israelites have too much time on your hands. From now on, no more straw will be given to the Israelites to make bricks. They will

have to gather the straw themselves," he ordered.

When Moses saw what happened, he called out to God. "Why did You send me to Pharaoh? Now the people hate me, for I have only made life worse for them."

God answered Moses, saying, "You will see how I will punish the Egyptians and how they will rush to send out My people from Egypt."

God's Miracle   וארא

God told Moses and Aaron to go back to Pharaoh.

"What miracle can you show me," the mighty king asked, making fun of Moses and Aaron, "that would make me want to let the Israelites leave Egypt?"

Without a sound, Aaron threw down his staff, and it turned into a snake.

Pharaoh called his magicians, and they too turned their staffs into snakes.

"Ha! My magicians are just as good as you," Pharaoh boasted.

But suddenly Aaron's snake swallowed up the other snakes and Pharaoh's magicians could do nothing to stop it.

"Get out of here!" Pharaoh demanded. He still did not believe that God had made this miracle.

The Ten Plagues

1. BLOOD

Pharaoh thought he would never see Moses and Aaron again. But the next morning, while the king was bathing in the Nile River, Moses and Aaron appeared again.

"Let my people go," Moses said, "or God will turn all the water of the Nile River into blood. All your fish will die and for seven days you and your people won't be able to drink from the Nile."

Pharaoh didn't believe Moses. So Moses said to Aaron, "Lift your staff and stretch your hand over the river." Everyone watched as all the water turned to blood. The Egyptian magicians brought water from their homes and turned it into blood too. But try as they might, they couldn't turn the blood back into water!

So all the Egyptians had to dig wells and try and find water, because for seven days the Nile River was a river of blood.

Yet Pharaoh, even after seeing all this, would not let the Israelites go.

2. FROGS

Moses and Aaron went back to Pharaoh.

"Let my people go," Moses said, "or God will make millions of frogs come out of the Nile River and jump all over the land."

Once again, Pharaoh wouldn't listen. So Aaron stretched his staff over the water, and millions, even billions, maybe zillions of frogs jumped out of the Nile River and into the houses, beds, sheds, pots, bowls, and even the ovens of the Egyptians.

Pharaoh's magicians could also make frogs appear, but they couldn't make them disappear! There were frogs everywhere!

"Please ask your God to take away these frogs," Pharaoh begged of Moses. "I promise to let the Israelites go."

But as soon as the frogs were gone, Pharaoh hardened his heart, which means he became stubborn and changed his mind. He would not let the Israelites go.

3. LICE

Moses and Aaron went back to Pharaoh.

"Let my people go," Moses said, "or God will send a terrible plague of lice throughout Egypt."

When Pharaoh wouldn't listen, Aaron stretched out his staff and hit the dirt. Suddenly, lice appeared everywhere, on everyone, on people and animals alike. Everyone was itching and scratching.

This time the magicians couldn't copy the plague. They too were covered with lice!

"Pharaoh! Pharaoh!" the magicians cried, "This is the finger of God pointing at us and telling us we must let the Israelites go."

But Pharaoh refused to listen, even to his magicians, and the plague of lice continued until God stopped it.

4. WILD BEASTS

God told Moses and Aaron to get up early one morning and meet Pharaoh at the Nile River where he was going to bathe.

"Let my people go," Moses said, "or God will send a stampede of wild animals all across the land — except in Goshen, where the Israelites live. These animals will attack anyone who goes outside, and they will destroy the land. Only the Israelites will be safe from the animals. This will prove to you that God wants you to send the Israelites out of Egypt."

When Pharaoh refused to believe Moses, God sent a stampede of wild animals racing throughout Egypt. Only the land of Goshen was safe from the wild animals. It was almost as if an invisible fence surrounded Goshen and protected the Israelites from the wild animals.

Pharaoh called Moses and Aaron to appear before him.

"Enough! Enough!" he yelled. "You can take the Israelites out of Egypt to worship your God. Only don't go too far away. You have to come back soon."

"Agreed," Moses said. "When I leave you today, I will ask God to get rid of the wild animals. But I'm warning you, don't try and trick me."

Moses prayed to God. But as soon as the wild animals disappeared, Pharaoh changed his mind again and would not let the Israelites go.

5. ANIMAL DISEASE

Then God told Moses to speak to Pharaoh again.

"Let my people go," Moses said to the king, "or God will send a horrible disease that will kill many of the Egyptian animals, but will not affect any of the animals owned by the Israelites."

Once again, Pharaoh refused to listen. So God made all the animals of the Egyptians sick. Yet not even one of the Israelite animals became ill. And even though Pharaoh saw what God was able to do, he still would not let the Israelites go.

6. BOILS

So God called to Moses, saying, "Take a handful of soot from a furnace and throw it high into the air in front of Pharaoh." Moses did as he was told and the soot spread across Egypt and infected the Egyptians with boils.

But even though these sores were very painful and ugly, Pharaoh still would not let the Israelites go.

7. HAIL

God sent Moses and Aaron early in the morning to meet Pharaoh at the Nile River again.

"Let my people go," Moses said, "or God will send the worst hailstorm ever seen by man. Any Egyptian or animal that is outside when this hailstorm comes down will be killed. Only the Israelites in Goshen will be able to walk around safely."

When Pharaoh refused to believe him, Moses stretched out his staff toward the sky, and immediately thunder and lightning appeared overhead. A deadly hailstorm crashed down on the land like a hammer banging on the earth. The hail was made of water and ice and snow...and fire! It smashed every tree and destroyed everyone and everything that was not inside.

Those Egyptians who believed God because of all the things they had already seen, brought their animals into their barns. But the rest of the people lost all of their animals.

Finally, Pharaoh saw that he was defeated, and he called for Moses and Aaron.

"I have sinned. Please ask your God to forgive me and I will let you go."

Moses agreed, but he said to Pharaoh, "Even though God will stop the hailstorm, I know you won't keep your word. Just remember, there are even worse things that can happen."

Sure enough, the minute the hail stopped, Pharaoh changed his mind again, and refused to let the Children of Israel go.

8. LOCUSTS　　בא

Moses and Aaron went back to Pharaoh and said, "Why are you too proud to admit that God is greater than you? Let our people go! If you don't, God will bring a plague of locusts across the land to eat anything that the hail didn't destroy. These locusts will invade every inch of your land and your houses. Believe us, you have never seen anything like this!"

By this time, even Pharaoh's servants realized that Egypt would be destroyed unless Pharaoh listened to God. "Please," they pleaded, "let the Israelites go!"

Pharaoh saw that his people were afraid of the God of the Israelites, so he said to Moses, "If I let you go, whom will you take with you?"

"We'll take everyone," Moses told the king, "men, women, children, old people — even our animals!"

"You may take the men only," Pharaoh insisted. "Let them go into the desert and serve your God, but everyone else stays here."

Moses realized that Pharaoh was still not ready to let the Israelites go. So he held up his staff, and a mighty wind came from the east and brought a thick cloud of locusts. There were so many locusts that they blocked out the noonday sun and made the sky as dark as night! The locusts ate and ate and ate. They ate everything that had not been destroyed by the fiery hail.

"I have sinned! I have sinned!" Pharaoh shouted to Moses and Aaron. "Just pray to your God to get rid of the locusts and I will let everyone do as they please! Hurry!" This time everyone thought the king really meant it, for the locusts had eaten everything, even Pharaoh's food.

So Moses prayed to God. A strong west wind came and blew all the locusts out to sea, until there was not one locust left in all of Egypt.

But as before, Pharaoh changed his mind, and would not let the Israelites go.

Would he ever learn from his mistakes?

9. DARKNESS

God told Moses to stretch out his hand toward the sky, and as he did so, a thick, heavy darkness covered the land of Egypt. It was so thick and so heavy that people could not see one another — they could not even move. This darkness went on for three days. But in the land of Goshen, where the Israelites lived, the houses were filled with light.

Pharaoh called for Moses and Aaron to come to him. "Go!" he commanded. "Go serve your God. Take everyone with you. Only leave your animals here."

"That won't do," Moses told him. "We need to take all of our animals with us to serve God, because we don't know which animals God wants us to sacrifice."

Pharaoh became very angry. "What? Are you arguing with me — the great Pharaoh, king of all Egypt? Get out of here! Now! If I ever see your face again, I'll have you killed!"

"As you wish," Moses answered, and he and Aaron left the palace.

10. DEATH OF THE FIRSTBORN

"There is still one more plague that I will bring on Egypt," God told Moses. "Then Pharaoh will finally let My people go. In fact, he will beg you to leave! But first, tell the Israelites to go to their Egyptian neighbors and get back all of the jewels and silver and gold that the Egyptians had taken from them in the past."

Moses told the Israelites what to do. The Egyptians were more than happy to give the Israelites anything they wanted. By now, the Egyptians were scared and just wanted the Israelites to leave. They would pay anything to get them out of Egypt.

Moses went back to Pharaoh and said, "Listen Pharaoh, at about midnight on the fifteenth of this month, Nissan, God will go through Egypt and destroy all the firstborn sons of the Egyptians — including your own firstborn son. Even the firstborn of the animals will be destroyed!

"There will be terrible crying and screaming among your people. But it will be quiet in the homes of the Israelites, not even a dog will bark. All the Israelites will be safe. And then, not only will you let us go, but you and your people will beg us to leave Egypt!"

Before Pharaoh could answer, Moses left the palace.

The First Passover

Moses had a great deal to do. God told him that the month of Nissan would be the month that the Israelites would leave Egypt. They would always remember this month as the time of their freedom.

But first, God commanded every family to roast a lamb and eat it. Later, as they were rushing out of Egypt, they baked *matzah*, which is bread that has not had time to rise. And they had to eat some bitter vegetables to remind them that although they were going to be free, they had been through very bitter times. This meal would be the first Passover Seder.

On that first Passover, the Israelites had to make a mark on their doors with some of the lamb's blood. This was a special sign between the Israelites and God. When God came to destroy the firstborn children, God *passed over* the houses of the Israelites and went to the Egyptian houses. That's why we call this holiday Passover, or *Pesach*, in Hebrew.

God then told the Israelites to celebrate Passover for seven days every year. People who live outside of Israel celebrate Passover for eight days. No foods with yeast, the ingredient that makes dough rise, are allowed to be found in the house on Passover. Matzah is the only kind of bread permitted during this time.

While the firstborn sons of the Egyptians were being killed by God, Pharaoh called for Moses and Aaron.

"No more!" Pharaoh cried. "Take everyone, everything, your families and your animals. Just leave! But please, bless me. Tell your God to spare me, for I am a firstborn too!"

So, after 430 years in Egypt, the Israelites packed their belongings, took the gold and silver and jewels, which the Egyptians were only too happy to give them, and raced out of Egypt.

More than a million Israelites left Egypt (over 600,000 men alone!). God's words to Abraham, that his descendants would be as many as the stars in the sky, were coming true. There were even Egyptians who tagged along because they believed that God would watch over them if they stayed with the Israelites.

God told Moses to tell the Israelites, "From this day, your firstborn sons and firstborn animals will be special to Me, because I

spared them from the plague in Egypt, by passing over the houses of the Israelites.

"This day will also be special to you and your children, forever. Even when you enter the land which I have promised to give your fathers, you will keep this holiday of Passover. It will always be a sign between Me and you.

"Now, write down how I took you out of Egypt. Then put these words inside two small boxes. One box you will wear on your arm, and the other between your eyes. These boxes will be a sign that you are special to Me and that I am special to you."

Today, we call these boxes *tefillin*.

Splitting The Red Sea בשלח

As the Israelites were preparing to leave Egypt, Moses took the bones of Joseph with him. In this way the Israelites were able to keep the promise they had made to Joseph to bury his bones in the land of Israel.

The Israelites travelled through the desert. God sent a tall pillar of cloud to lead them in the daytime, and a tall pillar of fire to lead them at night. But instead of marching straight to Canaan (the land of Israel), the Israelites were led by the pillars on a curvy path that sometimes even went back toward Egypt!

"They are lost!" Pharaoh announced when he heard that the Israelites were wandering through the desert. "What fools we were to have let them go. After them!" he shouted.

His generals gathered all the chariots in Egypt and, with Pharaoh in the lead, raced after the Israelites.

The Israelites looked behind them and saw the Egyptian army coming closer and closer. In front of the Israelites was the Red Sea.

"Where are we to run?" they asked one another.

Then they turned to Moses, fear and anger in their voices. "Why did you bother to take us out of Egypt? Now we will be destroyed by Pharaoh's army out here in the desert! Didn't we tell you to leave us alone? Isn't being a slave better than dying?"

"Don't be afraid," Moses answered calmly. "You don't

have to do anything. God will protect you. Look at the Egyptians," Moses said. "This will be the last time you will see them alive."

Then Moses began to pray, but God told him, "This is not the time for prayer. You are the leader. Lift up your staff and stretch your hand towards the waters in front of you. Watch as the waters of the Red Sea divide!"

God moved the pillar of cloud behind the people so that it stood between the Egyptians and the Israelites. The cloud grew black and the Egyptians could no longer see the Israelites. Meanwhile the pillar of fire appeared in front of the Israelites, lighting their way.

The waters of the Red Sea rose up and split, leaving a path of dry land for the Israelites to walk on. All night the Israelites walked through the sea. The Egyptians followed close behind. By daybreak, the Israelites had reached the other side of the sea. The Egyptian charioteers were rushing to get to the other side too, but the ground under them suddenly turned to mud and the wheels of the chariots became stuck. Now it was the Egyptians' turn to be scared.

"Let's run away," they shouted to each other. "Their God is fighting for them. We can't possibly win."

Then Moses stretched his hand towards the water again and with a great "WHOOSH!" the waters came down upon the Egyptians.

The Israelites all stood on the shore, safe and dry. They watched as the waters rolled and churned, until all of Pharaoh's mighty warriors drowned in the Red Sea. Not one of them survived.

At last, the Israelites knew that there was nothing more to fear from Pharaoh and his army. The people could see the great strength of God, and the miracle that God had performed for them. And they believed in God and in God's servant, Moses.

A Special Song

Then Moses and the Israelites sang a song to God.

I will sing to God,
 For he has won the battle.
The Egyptian soldiers have been
 Thrown into the sea.
God is my strength,
 And saves me.
God has fought my battle for me,
 And has drowned Pharaoh's
 soldiers.
Anyone who tries to conquer God
 Will certainly be destroyed.
When the Egyptians said:
 "Attack the Israelites!"
God made the wind close up the sea,
 And the Egyptians were covered
 with water.
Who is like You, God?
 You have led us out of Egypt!
The other nations will hear of this,
 And they will tremble with fear.
We know You will take us
 to the place You promised,
 The holy place You
 have created for us.
God is King of
 everything forever!

Then Miriam, the sister of Moses and Aaron, began to sing a song to God, thanking God for saving her people. And all the women of Israel played music and danced to show their joy.

Bitter Water

Moses led the Israelites away from the sea, into the desert. They travelled for three days, always looking for fresh water. Finally, they came to a place called Marah, which means bitter in Hebrew, and indeed, the water there was very bitter, much too bitter to drink.

The people ran to Moses, complaining. "What should we drink?" they asked.

Moses prayed to God. Just then, a tree appeared in front of him, and Moses threw it into the bitter water. Miraculously, the water turned sweet.

Then God gave the people more laws and said, "If you follow My laws, I will always be your healer and keep you safe from the diseases that plagued the Egyptians."

Manna In The Desert

In the second month of their travels through the desert, the matzah that the Israelites had brought with them ran out. Once again, the people began to complain.

"Moses and Aaron, did you take us out of Egypt just to bring us into the desert to die? At least in Egypt we had plenty of bread and meat to eat!"

Moses prayed to God for guidance. God said, "Tell the people that I will send them food from the heavens. Every morning they will be able to go outside their tents and pick up the food and it will taste delicious.

But they should pick up only enough food for that day. They should not try to save any for the next day.

"On Friday, however, tell them to pick up a double portion of food to last them through Shabbat. For on Shabbat they must not gather any food outside their tents. That which they gather on Friday will stay fresh through Shabbat."

But there was more.

"I have heard the people's complaints," God assured Moses.

"They want meat, and they shall have meat. Quail — a most delicious bird — will come to the camp at night and the people will catch them easily and eat them. In this way, the people will have all the food they have asked for."

The next morning a layer of dew formed on the ground, and upon it came down a white shimmering food that looked like a pancake. On top of the pancake appeared another layer of dew. In this way no sand could touch the food. When the sun's rays evaporated the top layer of dew, the Israelites came out and looked around.

"What is this?" they asked each other, pointing to the pancakes.

"It looks like a portion of some sort of food," one person suggested. In those days, the Hebrew word for "a portion of food" was *mahn*. In English, we call the food they found in the desert, manna.

Then Moses told the people that this was food from God, so they went out to collect it.

But some people were greedy, and didn't believe Moses. They were afraid there would not be any manna the next day. They took extra manna and tried to keep it overnight. But in the morning, everything they had taken was full of worms and completely rotten. On Friday, everyone took a double portion of manna. Again, some people didn't believe Moses and went out to look for manna on Shabbat too, but they didn't find any.

"Remember what I told you," Moses reminded them, "that just as Shabbat is a holy day for God, it is also a holy day for us. We cannot work on Shabbat, even to get food."

Then Moses told Aaron to take a jar and put some manna in it, so that in the future when people would see the manna, they would know that God had sent special food from heaven for the Israelites.

And during their 40 years in the desert, the manna came down every day, except on Shabbat.

Water From A Rock?

The people continued travelling through the desert. It was very, very hot and they were running out of water.

"What have you done to us, Moses?" the Israelites complained again. "Do you want our children to die here in the desert?"

Moses turned to God. "Look at them, God," he said. "In another second they will stone me if I don't give them water!"

Then God said, "Take your staff and go with the leaders of the people to a place I will show you. There you will hit a rock and water will pour out of the rock, and the people will be able to drink from the water as if it were a spring."

Moses did as God commanded and hit the rock in front of the leaders of the people, and fresh water poured out of it.

The Israelites called the place Massah and Meribah, which in English means "testing and arguing," because in this place they tested God's patience and argued with Moses.

The Enemy Amalek

The Amalek nation was very strong. When they heard that the Israelites had escaped from Egypt and were resting in Rephidim, the area where Moses had hit the rock, the Amalekites decided to attack.

Moses called to Joshua, his assistant, and said, "Go out and fight Amalek. Take our bravest men with you. I will go up to the top of that hill with my staff and help you win the war."

So, while Joshua fought Amalek, Moses went to the top of the hill with Aaron and Hur, Miriam's son. The battle raged. Whenever Moses held up his hands, the Israelites started winning, but when he became

tired and dropped his hands, they began to lose the battle. Finally, Aaron and Hur put a rock under Moses so he could sit down. Then Aaron took one of Moses' hands and held it up high, while Hur took the other hand and did the same. By the time the sun began to set, Joshua and the Israelites had defeated the Amalek army.

After the battle, God said to Moses, "Write down what I say to you, and make sure Joshua knows it well: I promise that someday I will wipe out the nation of Amalek."

From God's words, Moses understood that the battle with Amalek would go on from generation to generation because Amalek would always be the sworn enemy of the Children of Israel.

Moses Appoints Judges   יתרו

Moses had married Tzipporah, the daughter of Yitro, who was from the nation of Midyan. Moses had left his wife and their two sons, Gershom and Eliezer, with his father-in-law. When Yitro heard all the miracles that God had done for the Israelites and that Moses was their leader, he brought Tzipporah and the children to see him.

Moses greeted them all very warmly. He was happy to see his family and he had great respect for Yitro.

The next day, Yitro saw people waiting in a long line for Moses to judge them. They had come to Moses for him to decide their arguments.

"Moses," Yitro advised his son-in-law, "what you are doing is too hard for one man. Pick some men you trust to help you. They will judge most of the problems that arise. The very serious problems they can send to you."

Moses thought that Yitro's idea was a good one and he did exactly as Yitro advised.

Mount Sinai

In the third month of their journey through the desert, the Israelites came to Mt. Sinai. Moses went up the mountain, where God told him to prepare the people to receive the Torah — the words of God.

"Tell the people," God said to Moses, "you have seen what I did to the Egyptians, and how I took you out of Egypt as if you were on the wings of eagles. Now, if you will listen to Me and obey My laws, then you will be a special people to Me. You will be a holy nation."

When Moses came down from the mountain and told the people what God had said, they answered, "We will do all that God asks of us! We will obey God's laws!"

Then God told Moses how the Israelites should prepare themselves to receive the Torah. There would be a boundary line at the foot of the mountain which they would not be allowed to pass. Everyone would have to wash their clothes and try to keep as pure as possible.

Three days later, in the early morning, the people woke up to the sound of loud claps of thunder.

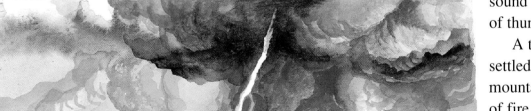

A thick cloud settled on top of the mountain and tongues of fire shot out of the cloud. Mount Sinai itself began to shake, and suddenly a shofar sounded loudly throughout the camp. Moses led the people to the foot of the mountain, and they shivered and trembled at what they saw.

Then God spoke:

The Ten Commandments

I am the Lord your God, who took you out of the land of Egypt, out of slavery.

You must never have any other gods. You must never make any idols, neither from My creations like the sun and the moon, nor from creatures you make up yourselves. Never bow down or serve any idol, because if you do then I will punish you severely.

Never use My name to swear for no reason.

You must remember the Shabbat and keep it holy. You should work for six days of the week, but on Shabbat stop working. And don't permit anyone in your family to work, not even your animals. This is because for six days I made the heavens and the earth, and everything in them. Then on the seventh day I took time off from creating, and I blessed that day, Shabbat, and made it holy.

Honor your father and mother, and I will give you long life.

Do not murder.

Do not get involved with a woman who is married to someone else.

Do not steal.

Do not swear in court that you saw or heard something, if it's not true.

Do not become jealous of what other people have.

So much was happening at once — the thunder, the lightning, the shofar, the voice of God!

"Please, Moses," the people cried as one. "It is too much for us to hear God speak. Please ask God to talk to you and you will tell us what the Torah says."

And so Moses stayed on the mountain and God gave him all the laws that the people would need to live by.

משפטים The Laws Of The Torah

These are some of the many laws which God told Moses:

If someone kills a person by accident, he can run to a "city of safety" so that no one will take revenge on him.

If someone kills a person on purpose, he will not be allowed into a "city of safety."

If someone kills a person, he must stand trial for murder.

If someone kidnaps a person and sells him into slavery, the kidnapper will stand trial like a murderer.

If someone beats up his mother or father he will stand trial like a murderer.

If someone beats up another person, then he has to pay for the time that that person couldn't work and for his doctor's bills.

If someone knocks out another person's eye or tooth, then he has to pay for what he did.

If someone curses his parents with a curse that includes the name of God, he will stand trial like a murderer.

If someone lets his animal graze in another person's field, he must give the owner the best produce from his own fields in return.

You must respect God, your leaders, and judges. Do not curse them.

If someone digs or uncovers a pit in a public road, and another person's animal falls into the pit and dies, then the one who dug or opened up the pit has to pay the owner of the animal.

If there are strangers who live among you, you must treat them well, and not hurt them or steal from them. Remember that you were once strangers in the land of Egypt.

Do not judge in favor of a man just because he is poor.

If you find your friend's animal wandering on the road, you must return it to him.

Be especially nice to widows and orphans.

Do not listen to lies.

If you are judging between two people, don't take any gifts from either person, because then you won't be able to judge fairly.

You cannot eat any animals that are found dead in the field. Give them to the dogs instead. If you want to eat an animal, you must kill it in a kosher way before you can eat it.

The Four Watchers

A) THE ASKER

Zoe *asks* her neighbor, Harriet, to do her a favor and watch some money for her. When Zoe asks for the money back, Harriet says it was stolen. If no robber is found, Harriet has to go to court and swear that she did not take the money for herself. Once Harriet swears, she is believed, and Zoe will have to wait for the robber to be found.

B) THE PAYER

Henry *pays* Donald to watch Jasmine, his pet dog. If the animal gets hurt or dies or wanders away while he is watching it, Donald must swear that it was not his fault. But if the animal was stolen from Donald while he was watching it, he must pay the owner for its value, unless the thief is found.

C) THE BORROWER

Danielle *borrows* Sandy's pet cat to chase away some mice. If the cat gets hurt or dies, Danielle must pay Sandy the value of the cat. But if Sandy was there when the cat got hurt, then Danielle does not have to pay.

D) THE RENTER

Alex *rents* Marty's pony for his son's birthday party. If the pony is stolen, then the court will decide whether, according to the agreement, Alex can just swear he didn't take the pony, or whether he has to pay Marty for it.

The Mishkan

תרומה

While Moses was on Mt. Sinai, he was told that it was time to build a special house for God, called a *mishkan.* Anyone who wanted to give gifts to help build the mishkan was welcome to do so. These gifts of gold, silver, brass, red and purple yarns, fine linens, oils, spices, and precious stones were called *terumah.*

THE HOLY ARK

The Ark was a big box made of wood and covered with a layer of gold inside and outside. Long wooden poles, also covered with gold, fit into special rings on the side of the Ark so that it could be carried through the desert.

The tablets on which were written the Ten Commandments were kept inside the Ark. On top of the Ark was what looked like a gold crown and on top of this crown were two golden Cherubim, figures like angels, with open wings and baby faces. These were the only human images allowed in the mishkan.

After the Ark was built, God spoke to Moses from the top of the Ark, between the two Cherubim.

THE TABLE

"Make a special table," God commanded Moses. "Make it from wood, and cover the wood with gold. Make a crown around the table and wooden poles coated with gold with which to carry the table. Make baking utensils, also from gold. On this special table put a stand with twelve loaves of bread. These loaves will last from one Shabbat to the next without spoiling."

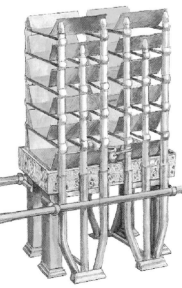

THE MENORAH

"Make a special menorah," God continued. "It should be made of pure gold. It should have seven branches. Six of its branches should come out from the middle branch, three from one side and three from the other side. And there should be gold flowers and bulbs and four bowls that look like almonds, decorating the menorah exactly as I show you."

THE MISHKAN

Then God showed Moses how to build the mishkan.

"Use strong wooden pillars and attach them to each other. Weave strong cloth around the outside of the pillars. Use the animal skins that people give you, to cover the mishkan. Then weave a giant rug, called a *pahrochet*, and hang it where I show you inside the mishkan. This will separate the inside of the mishkan, called the Holy of Holies, from where I will talk to you, from the outside of the mishkan, called the Holy, where sacrifices will be brought for the people."

THE BRONZE ALTAR

God showed Moses a long ramp with a tall, square table at the top of it. This was called an altar. This altar was to be used to help the people express joy or sorrow in a way that would make them feel close to God. If a person felt good about what God had done for him, or if he felt sorry for doing something against God's laws, he would take his animal and sacrifice it — give it as a gift — to God. Of course, only kosher animals could be used as a sacrifice. In those days, animals were very important to people. They could be used to buy things or to plow and harvest the land. So, if someone was willing to give his animal as a present to God, it showed that he really cared for God and the Torah.

"Make an altar out of wood, and cover the wood with bronze," God told Moses. "This will be the Bronze Altar upon which you will sacrifice certain animals. Make it just as I show you."

The Eternal Light תצוה

God wanted a bright light that would burn forever, to light up the mishkan. This light would come from a lamp which burned the best olive oil and would last from one night to the next. Today, many synagogues have an eternal light in front of the Ark, where the Torah scrolls are kept, as a reminder of this special light.

THE PRIESTLY CLOTHING

Aaron and his sons had to be prepared for the work they would do in the mishkan. They would be the *Kohanim*, the priests, whose special job was to make sure that the sacrifices of the people were done correctly before God. They would spend all their time just working in the mishkan.

"Tell your brother, Aaron, and his four sons, Nadav, Avihu, Elazar, and Itamar, that they must wear special clothes when they work in My house," God explained to Moses.

"These are the clothes they must wear: pants, a long sleeved shirt, a hat, and a belt."

The Kohanim were not allowed to wear shoes or socks. Shoes and socks carry dirt, and the Kohen's feet and hands had to be clean at all times.

Aaron was called the *Kohen Gadol*, or High Priest in English. He wore eight pieces of clothing. In addition to pants, a long-sleeved shirt, a hat, and a belt, the Kohen Gadol also wore a robe with bells at the bottom, a sleeveless shirt, a square plate on his chest, and a gold band across his forehead.

The special square plate on his chest was called the *urim v'tumim*. It had 12 colored jewels in it. Each of the twelve jewels stood for one of the twelve tribes of Israel.

THE INCENSE ALTAR

There was another altar that God commanded Moses to have the people build. It was called the Incense Altar because when certain spices, called incense, were burned upon it, the air was filled with a wonderful smell. Every day Aaron was to burn the spices upon this altar, once in the morning and once in the evening.

כי תשא Counting The Israelites

While Moses was still on the mountain, God said to him, "When you count the people, make sure you don't count the person himself. Rather, let each person give a coin, a half shekel, and count the number of coins given. This is very important, so that there will be no plague among the people."

Moses was told to count only those men twenty years of age or older. The half shekels collected would be used for the mishkan, to help pay for special animal sacrifices which would bring forgiveness for the people's sins.

THE MISHKAN AND SHABBAT

Then God told Moses who would be in charge of building the mishkan:

"Bezalel, the son of Uri, the grandson of Hur of the tribe of Judah, will build My house. I will fill him with knowledge and great talent so that he will know how to build everything. And I will give him a helper, Aholiav, the son of Achisamach of the tribe of Dan. They will do all that I have commanded."

But God wanted to make sure that no one would think that building a house of God was more important than keeping Shabbat.

So God warned Moses, "Tell the people to be careful about keeping My Shabbat. For the Shabbat is a sign of love between Me and the Children of Israel. It is a holy day. It reminds them that it is I who make them holy. Remember, six days you can work all you want, but the seventh day is Shabbat, a holy day, and no work is permitted."

Then God gave Moses the two tablets upon which the Ten Commandments were written.

Sin Of The Golden Calf

Moses stayed on top of Mt. Sinai for a long time. Many of the people felt sure that something terrible had happened to their leader. They ran to Aaron, saying:

"Aaron! Help us! Who knows what may have happened to Moses? We are out here in the desert all alone. Without a leader to show us the way, we will all die! Help us! Get us a leader!"

Aaron was very worried when he heard this. He knew what they meant when they said, "Get us a leader!" They wanted Aaron to make an idol, exactly what God had said they were not allowed to do.

But Aaron had a plan.

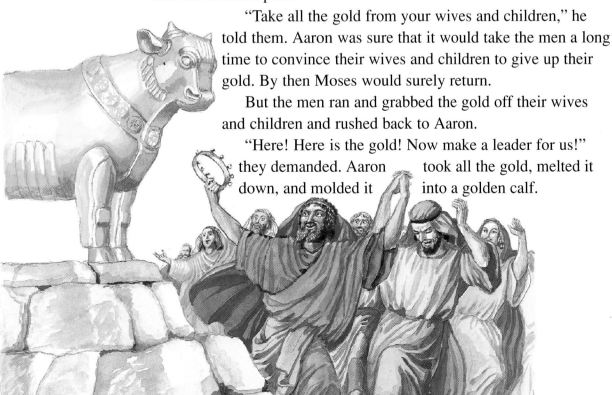

"Take all the gold from your wives and children," he told them. Aaron was sure that it would take the men a long time to convince their wives and children to give up their gold. By then Moses would surely return.

But the men ran and grabbed the gold off their wives and children and rushed back to Aaron.

"Here! Here is the gold! Now make a leader for us!" they demanded. Aaron took all the gold, melted it down, and molded it into a golden calf.

The people were happy and began yelling to each other: "Here is your god! Here is the god that took us out of Egypt!"

Aaron realized that what the people were saying was silly. They had just made this idol — how could it possibly have taken them out of Egypt? But the people wanted to believe in the idol. So Aaron said, "I will build an altar so that you can bring sacrifices. We'll have a big party tomorrow in honor of this god."

Aaron was sure that Moses would show up the next day. After all, Moses had told them that he would stay on the mountain forty days and nights. Now the time was up.

But the next morning, the people rose early and brought sacrifices to the golden calf, ate and drank, and had a big party. Moses still had not come.

MOSES DEFENDS HIS PEOPLE

"Moses, go down the mountain," God commanded. "A terrible thing is happening. The people are bowing down to a golden calf and saying that it took them out of Egypt.

"I see how these people act," God said angrily. "They are stubborn and not willing to obey My commandments. So, if you will agree, I will destroy them all and make you and your children the new Israelites."

Moses was horrified. Would God really do such a thing?

"God," Moses pleaded, very upset. "Don't be angry at Your people. After all, You took them out of Egypt and brought them this far. What

will all the nations of the world say? That God took them out of Egypt to kill them in the desert? Does that seem right? Please God, have mercy on Your people!

"Remember too," Moses added," that You promised Abraham, Isaac, and Jacob to make their children as many as the stars in heaven and give them a land of their own."

God liked the way Moses defended the Israelites. "I will do as you wish," God said, "and not destroy My people."

But of course, this did not mean that the troublemakers who convinced the people to sin would not be punished.

THE ISRAELITES ARE PUNISHED

Moses took the two tablets with the Ten Commandments on them and went down the mountain. As he came to the bottom of the mountain he met his helper, Joshua, who had been waiting for him. They both heard loud yelling and shouting coming from the camp.

"The people are being attacked!" Joshua declared.

"No," Moses answered, looking very worried. "This is not the sound of people attacking or people retreating from an enemy. This is the sound of people rebelling against God."

As they approached the camp, Moses saw the golden calf. The people were celebrating in front of this idol. Moses became so angry that he threw down the two tablets and they shattered.

Then Moses rushed into the camp, took the golden calf, and melted it back down into gold. He ground the gold so that it became as fine as dust, spread the gold dust on water, and made the people drink it.

Next, Moses turned to Aaron.

"What did the people do to you that you allowed them to sin like this?" he asked his brother.

"Don't be angry, Moses," Aaron said. "You know how difficult these people are. What choice did I have? They thought you were gone and insisted that I give them a substitute."

Moses saw that the people had become wild and uncontrollable. They had to be stopped.

Moses stood at the entrance to the camp and declared, "Whoever is on God's side, come and stand with me!"

The entire tribe of Levi came forward.

Moses told the Levites, "You will punish all those who have bowed down to the golden calf, while I go up and ask God to forgive the people."

Moses Asks God A Great Favor

Moses went back up the mountain. He knew that after the awful way the people had behaved, God might still want to destroy many of them. But Moses was determined to argue with God in order to save all the Children of Israel.

"Please God," Moses said when he came to the top of the mountain. "I know the people did a terrible sin by bowing to the golden calf. But I beg of You, forgive them. And if You can't forgive them, then destroy me too. Erase me from Your Book of Life!" Moses felt he would rather die than watch the Children of Israel be destroyed, even if many of them deserved it.

God answered Moses, saying, "I will only erase those who have sinned against me. But I will do as you ask. Then I will take the people to their land."

When Moses saw that God was willing to listen to him, he decided to ask God for a favor.

"God," Moses began, "You told me to take these people out of Egypt and that You would help me when I needed it. I need that help now, God. And I need for You to show me Your plan for Your people.

I need to know that You have chosen them above all others."

God answered, "This too will I grant you. Because you are so special to Me, I will show you My plan."

Then Moses dared to ask God for the greatest favor anyone could ask of God. Moses said, "God, please let me see how You look!"

"Moses," God answered, "I am willing to show you My ways and how to call up My mercy when you need it. But I will not show you My face. For no one can see My face and live.

"Come Moses," God told him, "I will put you inside a crack in a rock and all that I do will pass in front of you. I will put My hand over your face, and when I take it away you will see My plan for your people. But My face you cannot see."

Afterwards, Moses went down the mountain. He was still so angry at the people for what they had done, that he took his tent and set it up outside the camp, to show everyone how upset he was. This tent was called the Tent of Meeting because it was here that God spoke to Moses, just like a person would speak to his friend.

The Second Ten Commandments

Now that the people were forgiven, God told Moses to make another set of tablets like the first ones. God would then write the Ten Commandments on these tablets as well.

Moses went back up Mt. Sinai, while the people waited for him. When he reached the top of the mountain and came close to God's

presence again, he heard God say, "I am God! Merciful, full of compassion, full of patience, full of goodness and truth. I reward people who do good things and punish those who do bad things. And the rewards I give always last longer than the punishments."

Then God commanded Moses to tell the people:

"When you come to the land of Canaan, I will destroy the nations in the land: the Emorites, the Canaanites, the Hittites, the Prizites, the Hivites, and the Yevusites. But don't think that when you have taken over their land you can do what you want. Don't make agreements with these nations and don't let your children marry their children. This will lead to idol worship and cause you great harm.

"When you settle on the land make sure to come up to Jerusalem three times a year — Sukkot, Pesach, and Shavuot."

Moses stayed with God for forty days and forty nights, just as he had done when he received the first Ten Commandments. But this time, when Moses came back down the mountain, the people were waiting for him and were happy to see him.

Moses walked down the mountain towards the people without realizing that a beam of light, like a bright white ray, was shining from his face. This light was so strong that the people couldn't look at him. They turned their heads away when he approached.

As soon as Moses realized what was happening he covered his face with a veil. When he spoke to God, he removed the veil. But when he spoke to the people, he kept the veil on.

ויקהל־ פקודי *The Mishkan Is Built*

Moses gathered the people together and told them about the mishkan that was to be built. First, he repeated the warning about not working on Shabbat. Then he told them what materials were needed to build the mishkan. The people were happy to give of their gold and silver and jewelry. They brought their finest materials, precious stones, oils, and

everything else that was needed. At dawn there were already lines of
people waiting to bring their donations. Instead of asking people to bring
more gifts, Moses had to tell everyone to stop bringing their valuables.
In a very short time Moses had collected more than was needed to build
the mishkan.

Great care and wisdom went into building the mishkan. People all
joined together with much joy and love. They were very careful to
follow all that God had said, down to the smallest detail.

When the work was done, Moses blessed the people.

Then the pillar of cloud covered the mishkan and the spirit of God
filled the entire place. Whenever the cloud rose and moved forward, the
people followed it, and when it stopped and settled on the mishkan, the
people set up camp.

And that's how the Children of Israel travelled through the desert for
forty years.

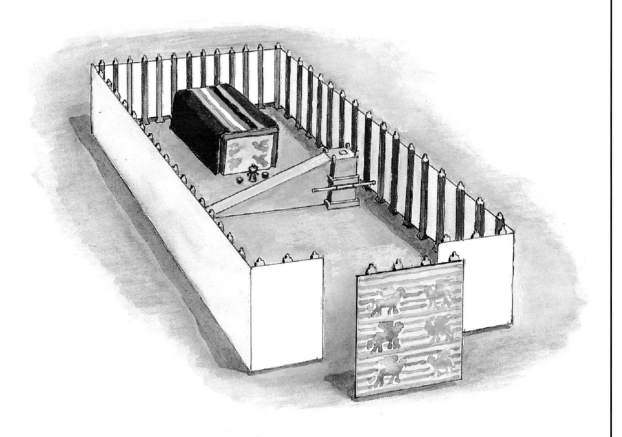

MIDRASHIM
TALES OF OUR SAGES

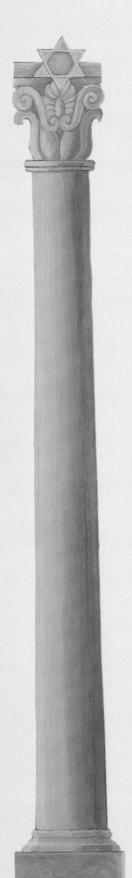

שמות

The Torah enumerates the seventy people from Jacob's family who entered Egypt. However, this number includes Joseph and his family – who were already in Egypt!

This teaches us that even though Joseph and his family lived within the immoral Egyptian society, they maintained the Jewish values that Jacob taught all his descendants.

When the Torah says, "A new king arose in Egypt," it means:

    This new Pharaoh was really a new king and never heard of Joseph and all that he had done for the Egyptians.

or

    This Pharaoh was actually the same king who had admired Joseph, but now that Joseph was dead, he preferred to act as though he had never heard of him.

At first, the Egyptians made the Children of Israel work *b'farech*. Usually b'farech is explained as "backbreaking work." But there is another explanation. If you split the word into two words you get *b'fah rech*, which means "with a soft mouth," or "with gentle words." And indeed, Pharaoh used persuasion to get the Israelites to do what he wanted.

How did Pharaoh get the Israelites to work for him? If Pharaoh had suddenly put them into bondage they might have rebelled and, as we know, Pharaoh was afraid of just such a rebellion.

So, Pharaoh had an ingenious plan.

At first, Pharaoh asked for volunteers to help build new cities and create monuments to the glory of the nation. He used rousing patriotic speeches to encourage them to work. In fact, Pharaoh himself molded the very first brick with his own hands. Then he took a trowel, and actually began to lay bricks.

Thousands of Egyptians who had come for the opening ceremonies of the new cities joined in, eager to contribute to the work. The Israelites also asked to be included in this project. That day, they worked as hard as they could – to show Pharaoh that they could work harder and longer than any of the Egyptians.

What they didn't know was that Pharaoh had sent his advisors to keep track of how many bricks each Israelite made. The next day, Pharaoh issued a proclamation requiring each Israelite to repeat the work he had done the day before!

In this way, Pharaoh enslaved all of the Israelites, except for the tribe of Levi.

When the Egyptians forced the Israelites to do "voluntary" work, the Levites were not included because they held a priestly position among the Israelites. That was something even the Egyptians could understand.

One hundred and thirty years after the Israelites came to Egypt, Pharaoh had a nightmare. In it, he saw an old man standing before him as he sat on his throne. The man held a balancing scale, with all the important people of Egypt on one side, and a little lamb on the other. Pharaoh was amazed to see that the lamb outweighed all the others!

He called to his servants and wise men, and ordered them to explain his dream. One of his advisers, Balaam ben Beor, had an explanation.

"This dream tells us that evil will come upon Egypt. A child will be born to the Israelites who will destroy the whole land, and kill all your people. Then he will lead the Israelites to freedom. You must do something to prevent this!"

Pharaoh's astrologers agreed and said that the child had been born on that very same day! "He is destined to die by water," they predicted.

One of his advisers then said, "Their ancestors have survived many different obstacles. But no one has ever tried to destroy them by water. Why not issue a decree that all newborn sons be thrown into the Nile River?" Pharaoh liked this idea.

So Pharaoh issued the decree. All males would be thrown into the Nile River as soon as they were born!

When Yocheved placed Moses' basket into the Nile, she knew what Pharaoh's astrologers had predicted. She was hoping that they would see that Moses was thrown into the Nile and thereby believe he was dead. And that's exactly what happened. As soon as Moses was placed into the river, Pharaoh's advisers came and told him that the redeemer of the Israelites had drowned. The decree was rescinded, and no more baby boys were killed.

The Midrash tells us that when Pharaoh's daughter saw the little basket floating in the middle of the Nile, she stretched out her arm, and a miracle occurred. It became long enough to reach the basket!

Yocheved kept Moses at her home until he was two years old. Then she brought him to the palace, where Pharaoh's daughter took over the role of his mother. God arranged for Moses to grow up in the palace so that he would learn how to behave as a leader and how to act in front of kings.

When Moses was only three years old, he was seated at Pharaoh's table at a royal banquet attended by many noblemen. Suddenly, Moses reached out his hand, took Pharaoh's crown from the ruler's head, and put it on his own head. The people were astounded!

"Look, he wants to be a king!" one man exclaimed.

"He will be a great leader!" shouted another.

"Perhaps he is the one the astrologers were talking about, the one who will free the Israelites!" suggested a third.

This troubled Pharaoh greatly. Just then, one of his advisers stood up. "The child is attracted to the glittery crown, as all small children are. Let us test him to see if he even knows what he is doing. We will place two plates before him, one with gold and one with burning coals. If he chooses the gold, I will agree that this means he does understand what he was doing when he took the crown and he must be killed. But if he takes the coals, it will prove that he does not understand. Why kill your daughter's young son for nothing?"

When young Moses was given a choice between gold and coals, he instinctively began to reach for the gold. But God made his hand move towards the burning coals. Moses picked up the coal and, feeling the heat, immediately placed his hand with the hot coal in his mouth.

Having burned his mouth from the hot coal, Moses had a problem speaking clearly for the rest of his life.

וָאֵרָא

The reason that Aaron, rather than Moses, called up the first two plagues was that both the plagues of blood and frogs came from the Nile River, which had saved Moses from death. Therefore, God would not ask him to use the Nile to punish the land of Egypt. Moses also did not bring about the third plague, lice, because the dust had hidden the Egyptian that Moses killed, and therefore it would have been wrong for him to hit the dust and turn it into lice.

The Midrash says that Aaron brought up only one giant frog from the Nile. But the people began to beat it, trying to kill it. Each time they hit the frog, it split into two. The more the people beat the frogs, the more they multiplied, until they filled the whole land of Egypt.

The plague of darkness lasted for seven days. It was almost impossible to breathe. During the first three days, the land was dark. Even the stars weren't visible. During the last three days, it got even darker. This darkness was thick too. If a person was sitting, he physically couldn't stand up, if he was standing, he couldn't sit down.

There were many Israelites who did not want to leave the land of Egypt with their brothers. They had become so Egyptianized they were not worthy of redemption. God decreed that these Israelites should die. But God didn't want the Egyptians to gloat over the death of Israelites by saying, "Look, the Children of Israel are dying too. They are also suffering from the plague of darkness." So, while the country was in darkness, and the Egyptians could not see anything, these wicked Israelites died and the surviving Israelites buried them.

While it was dark, the Israelites saw where the Egyptians kept their valuables. When it was time to leave Egypt, the Israelites asked the Egyptians to give them gold and silver. "Oh, we don't have anything like that," the Egyptians claimed. But the Israelites knew better. In fact, they knew exactly where to find these objects. "Sure you do," they insisted, pointing to the place the Egyptians had hidden their valuables. "They are right here!" And then the Egyptians would be forced to give them their valuables.

At the moment when God passed over the houses of the Israelites, all the idols of the Egyptians were destroyed. The wooden ones rotted, and the metal ones melted.

When the Israelites left the land of Egypt, they took Joseph's bones with them, just as their parents had promised Joseph long before.

בשלח

There were many miracles included in the splitting of the Red Sea. Here are a few of them:

- All of the waters in the whole world split at the same time as the Red Sea. Rivers and lakes, even the water in people's jars and cups split.

€ The sea was like a tent over the heads of the Israelites, protecting them from all sides.

€ The sea divided into twelve paths, one for each tribe. The walls of water were perfectly clear, like glass, so that the tribes could see each other.

€ When the Egyptian soldiers began to run onto the paths, the seabed turned into mud. Just as the Egyptians had made the Israelites work all day in mud, now they too were stuck in mud.

€ Many Egyptians fell out of their chariots and could not get up again. The most wicked were tossed up and down like straw, and suffered greatly before they drowned. Those who were a little better sank slowly. And the ones who were the least wicked sank quickly like lead and didn't suffer long.

The manna that fell on Friday, was different from the manna that fell on other days. It had a better taste and a better smell, too. The manna collected for Shabbat would not rot like leftover manna on other days.

The Hebrew word for manna is composed of two letters, *mem* and *nun*, the only nasal letters in the Hebrew alphabet. Hold your nose and say those two letters and you will feel their nasal quality. Similarly, the taste of the manna depended on its aroma. If a person had a cold and couldn't smell the manna, it had no taste. That's another reason why the Israelites called it mahn.

God told Moses to take the elders with him to the rock. He wanted witnesses to confirm that there had not been a well there all along. God also told Moses to use his staff. In this way the elders would see that the same staff he had used to bring about the plagues in Egypt could also bring about something good.

יתרו

When the Torah describes the way the Israelites moved from place to place in the desert, it uses the expression in the plural, "they travelled." But when the Israelites came to Mt. Sinai, the Torah says, "Israel camped," using the singular. This difference is due to the fact that when they arrived at Mt. Sinai the people were all united, without any hatred at all among them. They were living in complete harmony, and this was a sign that they were ready to receive the Torah.

Before God offered the Torah to the Children of Israel, God first asked the other nations if they wanted it. God did this so that the nations wouldn't be able to come later and say that they would have accepted the Torah if only it would have been offered to them too.

God first approached the children of Esav.

"What's in it?" they asked.

"You may not murder," God answered.

"Well, we could never accept that," they admitted. "Even Isaac's blessing to Esav said we should live by our swords. How could we possibly stop doing that?"

And they refused to accept the Torah.

Then God went to the children of Ishmael.

"What's in it?" they asked.

"You may not steal," God answered.

"We couldn't take a Torah that says that," they admitted. "We have to steal. That's the way we live."

Each nation that God offered the Torah to refused it for one reason or another. Finally God came to the Israelites.

"Do you want My Torah?" God asked them.

"Of course we want the Torah," they answered, without even asking what was inside it. "Whatever God says, we will do and we will listen."

So God gave the Torah to the Children of Israel.

When the mountains of the world heard that the Torah was to be given on a mountain, they all began to argue with each other. "Let the Torah be given on me," each one said.

The two greatest mountains in that part of the world were Mt. Hermon and Mt. Tabor. Both of these uprooted themselves and came all the way across the sea to Sinai, where the Israelites were camped. A holy voice rang out and asked them, "Why do you come here seeking the Torah? Don't you know that the Torah cannot be given on you? You are blemished."

Both mountains had come filled with boasting of their own self worth. "Since I am the greatest mountain," each one thought, "God will surely want the Torah to be given on me."

Mount Sinai, however, was the lowest and most humble mountain of all. Mt. Sinai didn't even think that God would choose it for this great honor. But that is exactly why God did choose Mt. Sinai. "This is the mountain where I want My Torah to be given," God said.

We learn that God considers excessive pride a blemish, and humility a good trait. A person who learns Torah needs to be humble so that he can learn from everyone, and not feel he has to show off what he knows.

משפטים

The Torah is very specific in teaching us how to behave with other people. If a person who is not Jewish converts to Judaism, we need to be especially kind and careful to him or her. If we get angry, we should never say, "You once worshipped idols." After all, they too can say, "So did your forefathers in Egypt. Do not look at your own wrongdoings in someone else!"

A Jewish slave who decides after seven years to stay with his master forever, rather than go free, must have his ear pierced. Why is this so? Because the same ear which heard on Mt. Sinai, "The Children of Israel are servants to Me (God) and not to man," dared to make himself a servant of a person forever.

תרומה

The mishkan was to be built through the donations of all the people, not just the wealthy. Whoever had the feeling in his heart that he wanted to give, would be able to give something, no matter how small the offering. And the collectors were not allowed to ask for donations, they could only take from those whose "hearts directed them to give."

The whole process of "giving" to the mishkan was really one of "taking." It can be compared to a person who brings a gift to a great king. If the king accepts the gift, the giver has more joy than if the king had given him a gift. He is grateful that the king actually accepted a gift he offered. That's how it is with God; a person receives much more than he gives.

Where did the Israelites get the wood to build the mishkan? Jacob saw through prophecy that the Israelites would one day need to build the mishkan. So before he went down to Egypt, he took with him saplings of some large cedar trees and planted them in Goshen. Before he died, Jacob told his children that when the time came to leave Egypt, they should take the trees with them. That is how they had wood when it came time to build the mishkan.

Cedar wood is very special and very strong, and it does not produce fruit. The Torah tells us that we are forbidden to use the wood of fruit trees for building. We cannot destroy those trees, even if it is to build a holy building like the mishkan or the Temple!

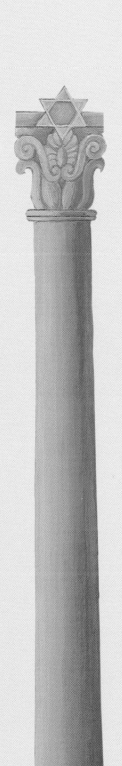

תצוה

When Moses saw all the Israelites bringing gifts to build the mishkan, he wanted to bring something too. But God told him, "Since they are bringing gifts because of you, you are on a higher level than the people. If one causes others to do good, he is on a higher level than they are."

God also explained to Moses that the donations were a way for the Israelites to atone for the sin of the golden calf. Since Moses had no part in that sin, there was no need for his donation.

The names of the twelve tribes were engraved on the jewels of Aaron's breastplate. But it was not permitted to carve the names with sharp tools which represent instruments of war. How then could this be done?

Moses used a special creature known as a *shamir*. Although it was a very tiny creature, it could cut through the hardest surfaces in the world. It could even cut right through iron. Moses had to keep it in large pieces of wool, inside a lead tube filled with barley straw. It would just eat through any other container.

Many years later, King Solomon searched very hard to find the shamir, so that he could use it to cut the stones used to build the Temple.

כי תשא

God wanted Moses to count the people. Each male over twenty gave a half shekel. But didn't God know how many men there were?

A person counts the things that he cares about. God loved the Israelites and counted them to show that they were as important as ever and that the sin of the golden calf had not lessened God's love for them.

When the Israelite men asked their wives for the gold they wore, the women refused to give it to them, not because they wanted to keep their gold, but because they would not be a party to idol worship. The men were thus forced to use their own gold rings to make the golden calf.

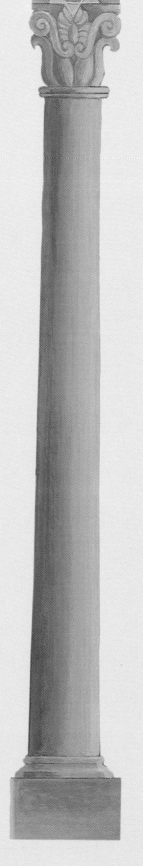

ଓଽଔ

The Israelites split into three groups at this time. The first group said to Aaron, "Make a leader for us!" This group believed in God, but felt lost without a leader. The second group shouted, "This is your god, Israel!" They actually worshipped the golden calf and 3,000 men from this group were eventually killed. The third group were the Levites. The entire tribe was loyal to Moses and refused to have anything to do with the sin of the golden calf.

ଓଽଔ

ויקהל

The people brought their donations to the mishkan early in the morning. We see from this that the Israelites were eager to give their presents and gave them with great joy and happiness. When a person is eager to do something, he wakes up early to do it.

ଓଽଔ

פקודי

When the mishkan was ready, and everything in it complete, it was time to set it up. But the boards were much too heavy, and every time the people tried to put it together, it fell down. The people came to Moses and said, "We have done whatever you told us to do but we can't get the mishkan to stand up."

Moses said to God, "How can any man put this together?"

Then God told him, "Moses, do not worry. I knew you were upset about not being able to donate to the mishkan. But now everyone will see that you have a major role in the creation of My house. You will be the one who erects it. Just put your hands on the boards and they will rise up themselves." Sure enough, as soon as Moses touched the boards, they stood up on their own and fit together. It seemed as if Moses was doing the work, but the mishkan really set itself up.

The Children's Haggadah

WHO KNOWS 15?

I KNOW 15!

15 are the sections of the Haggadah.

Did you know that 15 is a very **important** number in the Jewish religion because...

It represents the smallest number of letters that the Torah uses to write God's name: *Yud* and *Hey* – the letter Yud equals 10 and the letter Hey equals 5. Together they equal 15.

There are 15 different words that the siddur uses to describe the greatness of God. Many Jews say these 15 words right after the last paragraph of the *Sh'ma* prayer in the morning.

There were 15 steps from the men's section to the women's section in the Temple.

This last idea of *15 steps* is especially important for us. The 15 parts to the Haggadah are really 15 steps that help us understand what happened when God took the Jewish people out of Egypt.

As we move from step to step, see if you can figure out how each step helps us understand the Exodus experience, from slavery to freedom. If you have any trouble figuring it out, ask someone at the Seder. After all, asking is what the Seder is all about.

1 **Kadesh** קדש
MAKING KIDDUSH

2 **U'r'chatz** ורחץ
WASHING HANDS WITHOUT A BLESSING

3 **Karpas** כרפס
DIPPING A VEGETABLE

4 **Yachatz** יחץ
DIVIDING THE MIDDLE MATZAH

5 **Maggid** מגיד
TELLING THE STORY

6 **Rachtzah** רחצה
WASHING HANDS WITH A BLESSING

7 **Motzi** מוציא
FIRST BLESSING BEFORE EATING THE MATZAH

8 **Matzah** מצה
SECOND BLESSING BEFORE EATING THE MATZAH

9 **Maror** מרור
EATING A BITTER VEGETABLE

10 **Korech** כורך
THE HILLEL SANDWICH

11 **Shulchan Orech** שלחן עורך
THE PESACH MEAL

12 **Tzafun** צפון
THE AFIKOMAN IS EATEN FOR DESSERT

13 **Barech** ברך
BLESSING AFTER THE MEAL

14 **Hallel** הלל
PRAISING GOD

15 **Nirtzah** נרצה
ENDING OF THE SEDER

SOME BASIC RULES AT THE SEDER

When you drink wine or grape juice, lean to your left side. Lean
when you eat the matzah as well. Leaning to the side was a
sign of freedom in earlier times. Also, did you know that leaning
to the left side prevents you from choking on your food?!

Don't pour your own wine or grape juice. Have the person next to
you pour it for you. That's how people who were free did it at
the time of the Temple.

We drink 4 cups of wine or grape juice at the Seder. Only during the
meal do we drink anything else.

1 Kadesh קדש

Pour the first cup of wine or grape juice.
Lift up your cup and say the blessing.

בָּרוּךְ אַתָּה יי אֱלֹהֵינוּ מֶלֶךְ הָעוֹלָם בּוֹרֵא
פְּרִי הַגָּפֶן.

בָּרוּךְ אַתָּה יי אֱלֹהֵינוּ מֶלֶךְ הָעוֹלָם אֲשֶׁר
בָּחַר בָּנוּ מִכָּל־עָם וְרוֹמְמָנוּ מִכָּל־לָשׁוֹן
וְקִדְּשָׁנוּ בְּמִצְוֹתָיו. וַתִּתֶּן לָנוּ יי אֱלֹהֵינוּ
בְּאַהֲבָה (שַׁבָּתוֹת לִמְנוּחָה וּ)מוֹעֲדִים לְשִׂמְחָה
חַגִּים וּזְמַנִּים לְשָׂשׂוֹן אֶת יוֹם (הַשַּׁבָּת הַזֶּה וְאֶת־
יוֹם) חַג הַמַּצּוֹת הַזֶּה זְמַן חֵרוּתֵנוּ (בְּאַהֲבָה)
מִקְרָא קֹדֶשׁ זֵכֶר לִיצִיאַת מִצְרָיִם. כִּי בָנוּ
בָחַרְתָּ וְאוֹתָנוּ קִדַּשְׁתָּ מִכָּל־הָעַמִּים (וְשַׁבָּת וּ)
מוֹעֲדֵי קָדְשֶׁךָ (בְּאַהֲבָה וּבְרָצוֹן) בְּשִׂמְחָה
וּבְשָׂשׂוֹן הִנְחַלְתָּנוּ.

בָּרוּךְ אַתָּה יי מְקַדֵּשׁ (הַשַּׁבָּת וְ)יִשְׂרָאֵל
וְהַזְּמַנִּים.

בָּרוּךְ אַתָּה יי אֱלֹהֵינוּ מֶלֶךְ הָעוֹלָם, שֶׁהֶחֱיָנוּ וְקִיְּמָנוּ וְהִגִּיעָנוּ לַזְּמַן הַזֶּה.

Blessed are You God, King of the universe, who creates fruit of the
grape vine.

Blessed are You God, King of the universe, who chose the Jewish
people and gave us the commandments. Thank You for giving

us Shabbat and the Holidays, and especially this Holiday of Pesach, which is our Festival of Freedom.

Blessed are You God, King of the universe, who has given us life, and what to eat, and for letting us reach this season.

2 U'r'chatz ורחץ
WASHING HANDS WITHOUT A BLESSING

It is strange to wash hands without a blessing. Perhaps the reason is that we are like the Kohen during the time of the Temple. Just like the Kohen had to wash before sacrificing animals on the altar, so we wash before we begin the work of making a Seder at our table. Our table is like the altar in the Temple.

Perhaps this unusual law is meant to get children to ask questions. What do you think?

3 Karpas כרפס
DIPPING A VEGETABLE

Take a green vegetable, like celery, and dip it into salt water. Salt water reminds us of the tears that the Israelites shed when they were made to work so hard in Egypt. Did you know that vegetables were often dipped into liquids during the days of the Temple?

Say the blessing:

בָּרוּךְ אַתָּה יי אֱלֹהֵינוּ מֶלֶךְ הָעוֹלָם בּוֹרֵא פְּרִי הָאֲדָמָה.

Blessed are You God, King of the universe, who creates vegetables.

4 Yachatz יחץ
DIVIDING THE MIDDLE MATZAH

The leader of the Seder breaks the middle matzah and he puts the smaller piece back on the Seder plate. The larger piece is hidden by the Seder leader and the children try to find it. In some homes the children "steal" the afikoman and ask for prizes in return for giving back the afikoman.

5 Maggid מַגִּיד
TELLING THE STORY

Now we tell the story of Passover, or *Pesach* in Hebrew. The first thing we do is talk about the matzah. We begin by saying, "Look at the matzah. This is just like the matzah the Israelites ate in Egypt." Then, because we try to remember how terrible life was in Egypt, and how the Israelites were always hungry, we say, "If anyone is hungry, let him come to our Seder and eat." Finally, we express the hope that all the Jewish people will find their way to Israel. "This year we are here," we say, "but next year we want to be in Israel as free people in our own land."

Now pour the second cup of wine or grape juice. Don't drink yet!

THE FOUR QUESTIONS
What makes this night different than all other nights?

1) Is it because on all other nights we can eat regular bread or matzah, but tonight we can only eat matzah?
2) Is it because on all other nights we can eat any vegetable we want to, but tonight we have to eat a bitter vegetable?
3) Is it because on all other nights we don't dip our food even once, but tonight we dip our food twice?
4) Is it because on all other nights we can eat sitting or reclining, but tonight we all recline?

מַה נִּשְׁתַּנָּה
הַלַּיְלָה הַזֶּה
מִכָּל הַלֵּילוֹת

שֶׁבְּכָל הַלֵּילוֹת אָנוּ אוֹכְלִין חָמֵץ
וּמַצָּה הַלַּיְלָה הַזֶּה כֻּלּוֹ מַצָּה.
שֶׁבְּכָל־הַלֵּילוֹת אָנוּ אוֹכְלִין שְׁאָר
יְרָקוֹת הַלַּיְלָה הַזֶּה מָרוֹר.
שֶׁבְּכָל־הַלֵּילוֹת אֵין אָנוּ מַטְבִּילִין
אֲפִלּוּ פַּעַם אֶחָת
הַלַּיְלָה הַזֶּה שְׁתֵּי פְעָמִים.
שֶׁבְּכָל־הַלֵּילוֹת אָנוּ אוֹכְלִין בֵּין
יוֹשְׁבִין וּבֵין מְסֻבִּין
הַלַּיְלָה הַזֶּה כֻּלָּנוּ מְסֻבִּין.

THE ANSWERS

In order to understand why we do so many unusual things at the Seder table, we have to know a little bit about Jewish history. That's what the Haggadah is for. In Hebrew, the word *haggadah* means "to tell," and that's exactly what the Haggadah does — it tells us what happened to the Jewish people from the time they were in Egypt until they received the Torah at Mt. Sinai.

SLAVERY

When you are a slave, you are not your own boss. Usually you have to work so hard — and without pay — that you can barely take care of your family. That's what it was like in Egypt, until God took us out. Imagine — had God not taken us out, we Jews might still be slaves in Egypt to this very day!

A long time ago, five great Rabbis were sitting at the Seder table in B'nai Brak, a city in Israel. They were so involved in the Pesach story that they actually imagined themselves preparing all night to leave Egypt. The excitement of going from slave to free person — from being bossed to being your own boss — was so great that the five Rabbis talked about it all night. In the morning, they were still talking about this wonderful experience when their students came in to remind them that it was time to pray.

We too are supposed to get so caught up in the Passover story that we lose track of time.

THE FOUR TYPES OF CHILDREN

The Torah tells us there were four kinds of Jews who lived in Egypt when the Pesach story happened. Those four types of people exist today as well.

You can tell by the questions they ask as children, what kind of Jew they may grow up to be.

THE WISE CHILD ASKS:
"What are all the laws of Pesach that God has commanded you?"
THE PARENTS ANSWER:
"We will explain to you all the laws of Pesach during the Seder. For instance, at the end of the Seder you can't eat anything after you eat the afikoman because the last taste in your mouth has to be the taste of matzah."

THE WICKED CHILD ASKS:
"What are *you* all working so hard for?"
THE PARENTS ANSWER:
"God did so much for us by taking us out of Egypt. With *your* attitude, you would have been one of those Jews who died in the plague of darkness because *you* wouldn't have wanted to leave Egypt." This will anger the wicked child and perhaps make him think about what he has said.

THE SIMPLE CHILD ASKS:
"What's all this? Why the celebration?"
THE PARENTS ANSWER:
"God took us out from Egypt on this night, many years ago. And God destroyed our enemies and broke our chains of slavery."

The simple child will understand the battle with the Egyptians better than the laws of Pesach.

THE SHY CHILD:
He's really too shy to say anything.
THE PARENTS ASK AND ANSWER:
"You know why we do all this? We're at the Seder table to remember what God did for us by taking us out of Egypt."

THE PROMISE TO ABRAHAM

Where did the Jewish people come from?

Abraham was the first Jew. But his father, Terach, bowed down to idols. God took Abraham and brought him to the land of Israel, which was known as Canaan then. God promised Abraham many descendants and said that eventually they would be slaves in Egypt. God also promised to take the Jews out of slavery with great riches.

ENEMIES

So too, over the years there have been new enemies trying to destroy the Children of Israel. But God makes sure they don't succeed.

For example, Lavan pretended to like Jacob, but he really wanted to destroy him. He used tricks and threats but in the end — thanks to God's help — Jacob left Lavan's home richer and stronger than ever.

וְהִיא שֶׁעָמְדָה לַאֲבוֹתֵינוּ וְלָנוּ

שֶׁלֹא אֶחָד בִּלְבָד עָמַד עָלֵינוּ לְכַלוֹתֵנוּ

אֶלָא שֶׁבְּכָל־דוֹר וָדוֹר עוֹמְדִים עָלֵינוּ לְכַלוֹתֵנוּ

וְהַקָדוֹשׁ בָּרוּךְ הוּא מַצִּילֵנוּ מִיָּדָם.

EGYPT

Jacob and his family — 70 people altogether — went down to Egypt. In a short time they became a nation of many people. The Egyptians decided to make the Israelites slaves so that they could control them. They placed taskmasters over them and made life miserable for them. The Israelites worked day and night making bricks. It was backbreaking work and the people cried out to God.

God heard their cries and took them out of Egypt.

But first God punished Pharaoh and the Egyptians by sending them ten plagues.

Rabbi Judah put the Hebrew initials of the ten plagues together to make three words. This was an easy way to remember the names of the plagues.

דצ״ך עד״ש באח״ב
D'TZACH, ADASH, B'ACHAV

BLOOD	דם
FROGS	צפרדע
LICE	כינים
WILD ANIMALS	ערוב
CATTLE DISEASE	דבר
BOILS	שחין
HAIL	ברד
LOCUSTS	ארבה
DARKNESS	חשך
DEATH OF THE FIRSTBORN	מכת בכורות

כַּמָּה מַעֲלוֹת טוֹבוֹת לַמָּקוֹם עָלֵינוּ !

אִלּוּ הוֹצִיאָנוּ מִמִּצְרַיִם וְלֹא־עָשָׂה בָהֶם שְׁפָטִים **דַּיֵּנוּ.**

אִלּוּ עָשָׂה בָהֶם שְׁפָטִים וְלֹא־עָשָׂה בֵאלֹהֵיהֶם **דַּיֵּנוּ.**

אִלּוּ עָשָׂה בֵאלֹהֵיהֶם וְלֹא־הָרַג אֶת־בְּכוֹרֵיהֶם **דַּיֵּנוּ.**

אִלּוּ הָרַג אֶת־בְּכוֹרֵיהֶם וְלֹא־נָתַן לָנוּ אֶת־מָמוֹנָם **דַּיֵּנוּ.**

אִלּוּ נָתַן לָנוּ אֶת־מָמוֹנָם וְלֹא־קָרַע לָנוּ אֶת־הַיָּם **דַּיֵּנוּ.**

אִלּוּ קָרַע לָנוּ אֶת־הַיָּם וְלֹא־הֶעֱבִירָנוּ בְתוֹכוֹ בֶּחָרָבָה **דַּיֵּנוּ.**

אִלּוּ הֶעֱבִירָנוּ בְתוֹכוֹ בֶּחָרָבָה וְלֹא־שִׁקַּע צָרֵינוּ בְּתוֹכוֹ **דַּיֵּנוּ.**

אִלּוּ שִׁקַּע צָרֵינוּ בְּתוֹכוֹ וְלֹא־סִפֵּק צָרְכֵּנוּ בַּמִּדְבָּר אַרְבָּעִים שָׁנָה **דַּיֵּנוּ.**

אִלּוּ סִפֵּק צָרְכֵּנוּ בַּמִּדְבָּר אַרְבָּעִים שָׁנָה וְלֹא־הֶאֱכִילָנוּ אֶת־הַמָּן **דַּיֵּנוּ.**

אִלּוּ הֶאֱכִילָנוּ אֶת־הַמָּן וְלֹא־נָתַן לָנוּ אֶת־הַשַּׁבָּת **דַּיֵּנוּ.**

אִלּוּ נָתַן לָנוּ אֶת־הַשַּׁבָּת וְלֹא־קֵרְבָנוּ לִפְנֵי הַר־סִינַי **דַּיֵּנוּ.**

אִלּוּ קֵרְבָנוּ לִפְנֵי הַר־סִינַי וְלֹא־נָתַן לָנוּ אֶת־הַתּוֹרָה **דַּיֵּנוּ.**

אִלּוּ נָתַן לָנוּ אֶת הַתּוֹרָה וְלֹא הִכְנִיסָנוּ לְאֶרֶץ יִשְׂרָאֵל **דַּיֵּנוּ.**

אִלּוּ הִכְנִיסָנוּ לְאֶרֶץ יִשְׂרָאֵל וְלֹא בָנָה לָנוּ אֶת בֵּית הַבְּחִירָה **דַּיֵּנוּ.**

15 GOOD THINGS GOD HAS DONE FOR US

1) God took us out of Egypt.
2) God punished the Egyptians.
3) God destroyed the Egyptian idols.
4) God killed the firstborn Egyptians.
5) God gave us the Egyptians' gold and silver.
6) God split the Red Sea.
7) God led us across the Red Sea.
8) God drowned the Egyptian soldiers in the Red Sea.
9) God took care of us in the desert for 40 years.
10) God gave us the manna in the desert.
11) God gave us Shabbat.
12) God brought us to Mt. Sinai.
13) God gave us the Torah.
14) God brought us to the land of Israel.
15) God built the Holy Temple for us.

THREE SEDER SYMBOLS

Rabbi Gamliel said that if you don't explain these three symbols of the Seder you haven't done the Seder properly.

PESACH:

Why did the Jews eat the Pesach sacrifice in Temple times? To help them remember that God passed over the houses of the Israelites and killed the firstborn of the Egyptians.

MATZAH:

Why do we eat matzah? Because the Israelites did not have time to let the dough rise as they rushed out of Egypt. They didn't even have time to take extra food for the journey.

MAROR:

Why do we eat maror? Because the Egyptians made life bitter for the Israelites. The Hebrew word for bitter is *maror*.

WE MUST REMEMBER

We should not think that the Pesach experience is just a memory. We have to *feel* that experience. We have to feel as though we ourselves are preparing to leave Egypt.

Now lift up the cup of wine or grape juice and say:

לְפִיכָךְ

So we have to thank God for making all those miracles in Egypt. We have to bless God for taking us from slavery to freedom, from sadness to joy, from darkness to light.

Now put down the cup of wine or grape juice.

אֲנַחְנוּ חַיָּבִים לְהוֹדוֹת
לְהַלֵּל, לְשַׁבֵּחַ, לְפָאֵר
לְרוֹמֵם, לְהַדֵּר,
לְבָרֵךְ, לְעַלֵּה וּלְקַלֵּס
לְמִי שֶׁעָשָׂה לַאֲבוֹתֵינוּ
וְלָנוּ אֶת כָּל הַנִּסִּים הָאֵלֶּה:
הוֹצִיאָנוּ מֵעַבְדוּת לְחֵרוּת, מִיָּגוֹן לְשִׂמְחָה,
מֵאֵבֶל לְיוֹם טוֹב, וּמֵאֲפֵלָה לְאוֹר גָּדוֹל,
וּמִשַּׁעְבּוּד לִגְאֻלָּה. וְנֹאמַר לְפָנָיו שִׁירָה
חֲדָשָׁה - הַלְלוּיָהּ.

75

LET'S SING TO GOD!

A Song To God
We sing to You God!
Because You are high above all the nations,
And there is no one like You.
You help the poor receive food from the rich.
Women who can't have children pray to you,
And then they are blessed with children.

We sing to You God!
When the Children of Israel left Egypt,
The Red Sea split,
The earth trembled.
All this You did, God,
Even making water flow from a rock.

Now lift up your cup of wine or grape juice and say:

Blessed are You God, King of the universe, who took us and our fathers out of Egypt and allowed us to reach this night, when we eat Matzah and Maror. So too, allow us God to reach other holidays that will come during the year. Let these holidays come to us in peace and happiness as we happily do Your commandments. Thank You God for taking us out of Egypt.

Blessed are You God, King of the universe, who creates fruit of the grape vine.

Drink the wine or grape juice.

בָּרוּךְ

אַתָּה יי אֱלֹהֵינוּ מֶלֶךְ הָעוֹלָם
אֲשֶׁר גְּאָלָנוּ וְגָאַל אֶת אֲבוֹתֵינוּ
מִמִּצְרַיִם וְהִגִּיעָנוּ הַלַּיְלָה הַזֶּה
לֶאֱכָל בּוֹ מַצָּה וּמָרוֹר. כֵּן יי
אֱלֹהֵינוּ וֵאלֹהֵי אֲבוֹתֵינוּ יַגִּיעֵנוּ
לְמוֹעֲדִים וְלִרְגָלִים אֲחֵרִים
הַבָּאִים לִקְרָאתֵנוּ לְשָׁלוֹם. שְׂמֵחִים
בְּבִנְיַן עִירֶךְ וְשָׂשִׂים בַּעֲבוֹדָתֶךְ.
וְנֹאכַל שָׁם מִן הַזְּבָחִים וּמִן הַפְּסָ־
חִים אֲשֶׁר יַגִּיעַ דָּמָם עַל קִיר
מִזְבַּחֲךָ לְרָצוֹן וְנוֹדֶה לְךָ שִׁיר
חָדָשׁ עַל גְּאֻלָּתֵנוּ וְעַל פְּדוּת
נַפְשֵׁנוּ. בָּרוּךְ אַתָּה יי גָּאַל יִשְׂרָאֵל.

בָּרוּךְ אַתָּה יי אֱלֹהֵינוּ מֶלֶךְ הָעוֹלָם
בּוֹרֵא פְּרִי הַגָּפֶן.

6 Rachtzah רחצה
WASHING HANDS WITH A BLESSING

Wash your hands and say the blessing:

Blessed are You God, King of the universe, who gave us the commandments and commanded us to wash our hands.

בָּרוּךְ אַתָּה יי אֱלֹהֵינוּ מֶלֶךְ הָעוֹלָם אֲשֶׁר קִדְּשָׁנוּ בְּמִצְוֹתָיו וְצִוָּנוּ עַל נְטִילַת יָדָיִם.

7 Motzi מוציא
FIRST BLESSING BEFORE EATING THE MATZAH

Say two blessings before eating the matzah:

Blessed are You God, King of the universe, who brings bread from the earth.

בָּרוּךְ אַתָּה יי אֱלֹהֵינוּ מֶלֶךְ הָעוֹלָם הַמּוֹצִיא לֶחֶם מִן הָאָרֶץ.

8 Matzah מצה
SECOND BLESSING BEFORE EATING THE MATZAH

Blessed are You God, King of the universe, who gave us the commandments and commanded us to eat matzah.

בָּרוּךְ אַתָּה יי אֱלֹהֵינוּ מֶלֶךְ הָעוֹלָם אֲשֶׁר קִדְּשָׁנוּ בְּמִצְוֹתָיו עַל אֲכִילַת מַצָּה.

9 Maror מרור
EATING A BITTER VEGETABLE

Now eat some bitter vegetable and say:

Blessed are You God, King of the universe, who gave us the commandments and commanded us to eat maror.

בָּרוּךְ אַתָּה יי אֱלֹהֵינוּ מֶלֶךְ הָעוֹלָם אֲשֶׁר קִדְּשָׁנוּ בְּמִצְוֹתָיו וְצִוָּנוּ עַל אֲכִילַת מָרוֹר.

10 Korech כורך
THE HILLEL SANDWICH

Take some sweet Charoset and Maror and put them between two pieces of matzah and eat it. Don't forget to lean.

During Temple times the great Rabbi Hillel would eat a sandwich like this with maror.

11 Shulchan Orech שלחן עורך
THE PESACH MEAL

Now we eat the meal.

12 Tzafun צפון
THE AFIKOMAN IS EATEN FOR DESSERT

Eat some more matzah.

This is the last food that you eat at the Seder. From now on you can only drink.

13 Barech ברך
BLESSING AFTER THE MEAL

Pour the third cup of wine or grape juice.

Now say the blessing after the meal:

Blessed are You God, King of the universe, who gives food for the world. Because of You we have plenty of food and we hope that You will continue to give us all the food we need. Blessed are You God for giving food to the world.

Thank You God for giving the land of Israel to our fathers. Thank You too for taking us out of Egypt and out of slavery, and for giving us Your Torah and all Your Laws. We are very grateful for our lives and all the good things You have done for us, especially for the fact that You make sure we have food whenever we need it.

For everything You do for us, God, we thank You and bless You. We are fulfilling the commandment to thank You as it says in the Torah: "You should eat and feel full and bless God for the good land you have." So hear us when we say, Blessed are You God, for the land and for the food.

Make the blessing on the wine or grape juice:

Blessed are You God, King of the universe, who creates fruit of the grape vine.

בָּרוּךְ אַתָּה יי אֱלֹהֵינוּ מֶלֶךְ הָעוֹלָם בּוֹרֵא פְּרִי הַגָּפֶן.

Drink the third cup. Don't forget to lean.

Now open the door for Eliyahu (Elijah) the Prophet and say:

God! Let out Your anger at those nations that have hurt us and tried to destroy us. Make sure they are not around to hurt us any longer.

Pour the fourth cup of wine or grape juice.

14 Hallel הלל
PRAISING GOD

Now we sing the Hallel — the praises of God!

> We honor You God
> And we know You are the only God.
> Other nations bow down to idols of gold and silver.
> These idols have mouths, but can't speak.
> They have eyes, but can't see.
> They have ears, but can't hear.
> They have hands, but can't feel.
> We have God, and we trust in God.
> God helps us and protects us.
>
> Give thanks to God for God is goodness.
> When I call to God, God answers me.
> As long as God is with me, I have no fear.
> What can a person do to me?
> I know it is better to trust God than people.
> It is better to trust in the promises of God
> Than the promises of kings.

Give thanks to God for God is goodness,
God's kindness lasts forever.
Give thanks to God for God made the universe.
Give thanks to God for God took us out of Egypt.
Give thanks to God for God brought us into our own land.
Give thanks to God for God gives food to all living things.
God's kindness lasts forever.

Now we make the blessing on the wine:

Blessed are You God, King of the universe, who creates fruit of the grape vine.

בָּרוּךְ אַתָּה יי אֱלֹהֵינוּ מֶלֶךְ הָעוֹלָם בּוֹרֵא פְּרִי הַגָּפֶן.

Drink the fourth cup. Don't forget to lean.

15 Nirtzah נרצה
ENDING OF THE SEDER

God in heaven, make us a nation too numerous to count. Guide us, as free people to our holy city, Jerusalem. Hear us as we shout:

Next Year In Jerusalem!

Now we sing this special Pesach song:

WHO KNOWS ONE? אֶחָד מִי יוֹדֵעַ?

Who knows one?
I know one!
One is our God in heaven and on earth.

Who knows two?
I know two!
Two are the tablets of the Ten Commandments.

Who knows three?
I know three!
Three are the Fathers of the Jewish people.

Who knows four?
I know four!
Four are the Mothers of the Jewish people.

Who knows five?
I know five!
Five are the books of the Torah.

Who knows six?
I know six!
Six are the books of the Mishnah.

Who knows seven?
I know seven!
Seven are the days of the week.

Who knows eight?
I know eight!
Eight are the days for the Brit.

Who knows nine?
I know nine!
Nine are the months of pregnancy.

Who knows ten?
I know ten!
Ten are the Ten Commandments.

Who knows eleven?
I know eleven!
Eleven are the stars that were in Joseph's dream.

Who knows twelve?
I know twelve!
Twelve are the tribes of the Children of Israel.

Who knows thirteen?
I know thirteen!
Thirteen are the qualities of God that appear in the world.